ANIMALS
OF NORTH AMERICA

ANIMALS
OF NORTH AMERICA

TEXT BY LORAL DEAN

CHARTWELL
BOOKS, INC.

Published by
CHARTWELL BOOKS, INC.
A Division of **BOOK SALES, INC.**
110 Enterprise Avenue
Secaucus, New Jersey 07094

ISBN 0-89009-741-0

Produced by
Discovery Books,
70 The Esplanade,
Toronto, Ontario,
Canada M5E 1R2

Printed and bound
in Italy.

Designed by
Gerry Takeuchi.

The cougar or mountain lion
(*front cover*) is a master hunter,
stalking its quarry silently, by
night. Deer are its favorite prey.

Every spring and fall, huge
migrating flocks of snow geese
(*pages 2 and 3*) stop along the
banks of the St. Lawrence River.

Although black is their most
common color, black bears (*title
page*) sometimes are cinnamon-
colored.

Native to North America, the
hairy musk-ox (*page 8*) is a relic
of the last ice age.

Kodiak bears (*back cover*) can
weigh 2,000 pounds, more than
twice the weight of the average
grizzly.

CONTENTS

INTRODUCTION

When North America was first settled, the wildlife was so plentiful it seemed boundless. Great herds of bison, antelope, caribou and musk-oxen roamed the grasslands and tundra, and the endless forests that covered the land teemed with animals large and small. But toward the end of the nineteenth century, it became clear that unrestrained hunting and trapping could exterminate any species, no matter how abundant. In the twentieth century, public concern was sparked by conservationists such as the Englishman who adopted the name Grey Owl, resulting in the first effective conservation laws. In 1916, the United States and Canada signed the Migratory Birds Treaty to protect the millions of birds that migrate north and south of the border. Today, although not completely out of danger, wildlife does find sanctuary in national parks covering many thousands of square miles. Bison, once on the verge of extinction, are no longer endangered; more than 10,000 musk-oxen now thrive in the arctic tundra; after decades of decline, caribou are multiplying; and the moose, deer and beaver populations have increased.

Nearly 300 species of mammals, the dominant form of life in the world today, make their home in North America. As well, there are over 600 species of birds and hundreds of reptiles and amphibians. Our wildlife is as varied and remarkable as it is abundant. The shaggy, prehistoric musk-ox looks precisely like the relic of the ice age that it is. One hundred feet long and weighing as much as 145 tons, the blue whale, an inhabitant of the Atlantic and Pacific oceans, is one of the largest animals ever to have lived on earth. The Northeast's box turtle has been known to live 138 years, making it one of the longest living creatures in the world. The ponderous white pelican, a bird normally associated with the tropics, is at home rearing its young on the inland lakes. The largest bears in the world (polar, kodiak and grizzly), the largest deer (the moose) and the second largest rodent (the beaver), all are indigenous to North America.

North America encompasses vast variations in climate, geography and vegetation. Although much of the wildlife is highly adaptable to these variations, each animal seeks out its own ecological niche, depending upon its unique environmental requirements for shelter, food and reproduction.

This book presents these animals in their natural habitat. Here are the birds, seals, whales, sea lions, otters and turtles of the Atlantic and Pacific oceans and the familiar animals that are closest to home in woodlands, valleys, farmlands and meadows. Stunning photographs capture the variety of wildlife dependent upon innumerable inland water bodies and portray the mountain lions, goats, sheep, deer, bears and rodents that live in the mountains of the west. Here, too, is an introduction to the incredible mix of animals uniquely adapted to the rigors of life in the Arctic, the awesome polar wilderness that is the world's last great frontier.

Looking bewildered by the world around them, two young green-backed herons stand in their nest as they await the return of their parents. It will be some weeks before they join the adult birds in the business of gathering food.

THE SEA

The wildlife of the Atlantic and Pacific shores is a sociable group, swimming, hunting and breeding together in large packs and colonies. Each animal is uniquely adapted to these seas. Puffins and murres become airborne from drafts up the cliff faces of their seaside homes. Seals and whales have thick layers of fat to insulate them from cold water, while sea otters are protected by a lining of soft, plush underfur an inch thick.

During breeding season, these highly gregarious northern sea lions congregate in dense rookeries on rocky isles along the Pacific coast.

13

The massive northern sea lion is larger than any bear. An adult bull (*left*) can weigh up to one ton.

Atop an Atlantic cliff, a congregation of common murres attends a great cormorant (*above*) on her huge nest of seaweed and sticks.

The giant Atlantic leatherback turtle (*above*) is the world's largest turtle. It weighs about 2,000 pounds, not much less than its prehistoric ancestors.

Thick-billed murres (*right*) are large, ducklike seabirds. They inhabit rocky cliffs on the Atlantic and Pacific coasts.

Like their thick-billed cousins,
common murres breed in
immense seacoast colonies.

Each female murre lays a single
egg on bare rock. The egg is an
exaggerated pearshape so that it
will roll in a circle rather than
over the ledge.

Gannets (*left*), large, snowy
white seabirds closely related to
pelicans, nest in huge colonies
on rocky cliffs on the east coast.

Each female gannet lays one egg
in a cliffside nest (*above*) made of
seaweed. When they are 12 weeks
old, the young are left to fend
for themselves.

The common or Atlantic puffin feeds at sea on large schools of small fish, stacking as many as 40 in its big bill at one time.

Nicknamed the sea parrot because of its oversized, brightly colored bill, the tufted puffin (*above*) lives on the west coast.

The rare, beautiful osprey (*following page*), a magnificent, long-winged sea hawk, builds a massive stick nest high on a tree or crag. It lives entirely on fish, which it captures in its powerful talons after spectacular dives of up to 100 feet.

True monarch of the deep, the giant killer whale is a formidable foe. It is not unusual for 30 or 40 bold, rapacious whales to travel in a 'pod' while hunting.

Grey seals inhabit eastern coastal
waters. During the mating season, they crawl long distances
inland on deserted islands.

Prized by fur traders because of
its rich, lustrous pelt, the west
coast sea otter became almost
extinct. Now it is protected
worldwide.

The harbor seal lives in all off-shore waters and in some inland, freshwater lakes too. It enjoys romping in the surf and clapping its foreflippers with a loud splash.

FIELD AND FOREST

In the forests and on the open prairie, the endless cycle of birth and violent death is repeated among the creatures of the wild. Here the law of the wilderness dictates that the lives of predator and prey, hunter and hunted will be forever intertwined.

Sixty million bison (*left*) roamed the great plains of North America when the first Europeans arrived. Today only small herds of the shaggy beasts remain, most of them in national parks.

Much smaller than its cousin, the grey squirrel, the red squirrel (*above*) is rough, ready and rapacious, known for its boundless energy and cheeky chattering.

Bison are gregarious beasts, traveling in herds of four to twenty, which may be family bands. A bull (*right*) can stand six feet high and weigh a ton.

The shrill, nocturnal serenade of the coyote (*left*) symbolizes the spirit of the open prairie. Like its cousin the timber wolf, the coyote is intelligent and daring. But it is much smaller, weighing only 30 pounds.

The sprightly eastern chipmunk (*top*) is a friendly and familiar denizen of meadows, woods and cottage gardens.

Large, long-legged and long-eared, the white-tailed jack rabbit (*above*) can weigh up to 12 pounds, run 40 miles per hour and cover 20 feet at a single bound. Once nicknamed the jackass rabbit, it has the longest ears in proportion to body size in the animal world.

Like other members of the weasel
family, the tree-dwelling marten
is a savage, efficient killer, one of
the wildest creatures of the forest.

The raccoon looks like a fat cat and is almost as familiar. This masked bandit is bold and sociable, and eats anything, including city dwellers' garbage.

Graceful and swift, the prong-horn or prairie antelope (*follow-ing pages*) can run 60 miles per hour in short bursts. It is native to North America, with an ancestry of 10 million years.

Few animals dare attack the fear-some porcupine with its deadly armor of 30,000 quills. This cantankerous, lumbering creature can weigh as much as 25 pounds.

Bobcats (*above*) usually prey on small game such as muskrat, mink and beaver. But sometimes these lone, bold hunters kill deer.

The prolific eastern cottontail (*right*) produces four litters a year, but rarely lives for longer than six months because of its many predators.

With its magnificent, six-foot
wingspread, the turkey vulture
soars effortlessly, searching
for carrion prey.

One of North America's most common snakes, the harmless garter snake (*above*) is easily recognized by its stripes.

The black rat snake (*top*) can be eight feet long. A powerful constrictor, it feeds chiefly on rats, mice and other small rodents.

Dainty and delicate, the smooth green or grass snake (*above*) is attractive even to those who dislike snakes. Completely harmless, it feeds on worms and insects.

The melanistic garter snake (*above*) is often not recognized as a garter snake because of its color — all black except for its throat.

The western bullsnake or gopher snake (*left*) prevents millions of dollars of damage to crops by destroying harmful rodents like ground squirrels (gophers) and mice.

The pretty redback salamander is native to North America. It lives in damp, wooded areas, hiding inside decaying logs or stumps.

The land stage of the red-spotted newt (*left*) lasts three or four years. During this time, this attractive little woodland creature is called the red eft.

The eastern box turtle (*above*) has been known to live 138 years, giving it the longest lifespan of any wildlife species in North America. It lives in open woodlands, pastures and marshy meadows.

The timber wolf (*left*) is a cunning big-game hunter. His prey includes many animals larger and faster than he, among them the moose.

The gopher (*top*), whose proper name is Richardson's ground squirrel, is a common sight along prairie backroads.

Similar in coloring to the white-tailed deer, the inquisitive deer mouse (*above*) is North America's most widely distributed rodent.

The black bear is a solitary, quarrelsome animal, marking its home territory by clawing boundary trees.

Young, black bears are more
sociable than their elders. Above,
two half-grown cubs frolic in a
summer woodland.

The world's largest deer, the
moose can measure seven feet
high and weigh 1500 pounds.
This enormous, homely animal
feeds on huge quantities of twigs,
leaves and grasses.

North America's largest owl, the
lordly great grey owl (*above and
right*) flies with slow flaps of its
broad, rounded wings.

North America's largest and most exotic woodpecker, the pileated (capped) woodpecker (*above*) is the same size as a crow.

A little like a fluffed-up, giant chickadee, the curious grey jay (*left*) often haunts forest logging camps or picnic grounds in its search for scraps of food.

The hairy woodpecker (*above*) is easily confused with its smaller cousin, the downy woodpecker. It is common to most wooded areas.

Once dubbed the evil genius of the woods, the savage and powerful great horned owl (*far left*) preys on rabbits, rats, grouse, ducks, crows, skunks and even porcupine.

The world's tiniest bird, measuring only three inches, is the hummingbird. It is named for the sound made by its minuscule, rapidly beating wings. The rufous hummingbird (*above*), named for its rust colors, is most common in western North America.

Distinguished by its handsome, all-crimson head, the red-headed woodpecker (*right*) is a school-child's favorite art subject.

The flicker (*above*) is named for its familiar *wicka, wicka, wicka* call. It nests in tree trunks.

Second in size in the deer family only to the moose, the elk (*left*) once roamed across much of central North America. Now it is found only in protected areas.

61

The skunk is a first-rate marksman. If the wind is favorable, it can shoot its evil-smelling, musky fluid at an enemy as far as 20 feet away — with uncanny accuracy.

A familiar rural animal, the
woodchuck or groundhog loves
to sunbathe near its burrow.

A stout-bodied member of the
weasel family, the sturdy badger
is a powerful digger and a
courageous fighter.

With its muscular, serpentine body, the ferocious little ermine is a bold and agile hunter.

No one is certain of the origin of Sable Island's wild horses (*following pages*). About 200 of the small, stocky horses live on this windswept sandbar deep in the Atlantic Ocean off the coast of Nova Scotia.

Bigger than a bobcat, the lithe-bodied, long-legged lynx (*above*) stalks its prey at night.

North America's largest bat, the hoary bat (*far right*) has a wing spread of 17 inches. By day, it hangs in trees deep in the forest.

The snowshoe hare (*right*), named for its large, padded hind feet, is a social creature. As many as 25 have been seen gamboling in forest clearings on frosty, moonlit winter nights.

The grey squirrel (*left*) is a familiar, friendly resident of city parks and suburban gardens in eastern North America

The gorgeous, ring-necked pheasant (*above*), with its beautiful blend of colors and long, tapering tail, is the glamor bird of game species.

A fold of loose, furred skin extending from wrist to ankle enables the flying squirrel (*far left*) to glide from one tree trunk to another. Because these small acrobats are nocturnal, they are less familiar than other squirrels.

The red-tailed hawk (*above, right*) nests in trees or on cliff ledges, feeding its young small rodents like this groundhog.

Extraordinarily tame and inquisitive, the tiny saw-whet owl (*far right*) is the most charming bird in the owl family.

Contrary to its reputation as a sly, cunning animal, the red fox is shy and nervous. Preferring lakeshores, natural clearings and tundra areas to dense forests, red foxes inhabit most of North America.

The grey fox climbs trees,
jumping easily from branch to
branch. Unlike the red fox, it
prefers forests and marshes.

A master of camouflage, the long-eared owl (*above*) is named for its close-set ears.

In winter, bands of white-tailed deer (*right*) pack down favorite feeding grounds. The crowning glory of this slender, graceful animal is its tail, almost a foot long with a snowy white undersurface.

LAKES AND RIVERS

Great numbers of North America's birds, rodents, frogs, turtles and snakes rely on a nearby body of fresh water for their food and shelter. This is hardly surprising in a continent containing countless natural lakes, rivers, streams and marshlands, among them the largest freshwater lakes in the world.

Famous for its powerful, paddle-shaped tail, which it slaps against the water to signal danger, the beaver (*left*) is North America's largest rodent, weighing as much as 90 pounds.

79

The largest North American member of the rat family, the muskrat (*above*) is an amphibious rodent, building its house from cattails, sticks and mud.

The roguish belted kingfisher (*right*) with its ragged crest, dives headlong into the water to capture a fish in its powerful, pointed bill.

With its stately, slow-measured
flight, the great blue heron has
a commanding, elegant presence.

The great blue heron's nest
is a treetop platform of sticks,
sometimes located far from the
shallow marshland or lake
in which it feeds.

The majestic bald eagle (*above*), national emblem of the United States, has declined alarmingly in recent years because of hunting and pesticides. This great bird is seen mainly along the seacoast.

One of the world's fastest birds, timed at 180 miles per hour in a dive, the peregrine falcon (*far right*) is streamlined and powerful. It can kill its prey in mid-air with a single blow from its huge, taloned feet.

The handsome common loon,
famous for its wild, quavering
call, travels alone or in a single
pair on open water on deep lakes.

In its spring breeding plumage,
a showy golden horn on each side
of its head, the chunky horned
grebe is at its most elegant.

The river otter is at home
on land and water. It loves to
play, and spends hours gliding
down mud banks.

The handsome, ornamental mallard (*left*), adaptable and widespread, probably is the best-known duck in the world.

The aristocrat of wild geese, the Canada goose (*above*) mates for life and is a formidable defender of its nest and young.

Although white pelicans (*following pages*) usually are associated with salt water and the tropics, they also nest in large colonies on freshwater lakes.

The ponderous white pelican,
with its great pouched beak, flies
with an easy, unhurried grace,
alternately gliding and flapping
in almost perfect unison with
the flock.

Mergansers, named for their slender, cylindrical bills, are fish-eating, diving ducks. The handsome, hooded merganser (*above*) is the smallest and least common of them.

With its needlelike, upwardly curving bill, which it sweeps from side to side to snap up food, the American avocet (*right*) is an unmistakable sight along marshes and lakeshores.

A member of the heron family,
the little snowy egret is a wading
bird seen at the edges of freshwater marshes, ponds and bays.

A waterbird as big as a gull, the Caspian tern (*above*) fishes by making powerful dives.

Shy and wary, the map turtle (*left*) likes to sunbathe on a rock or log with a view, the easier to topple into the water at a moment's notice.

The spiny softshell turtle (*above*) sometimes is called the flapjack or pancake turtle because of its unusual, leathery shell. Softshell turtles split off from their hard-shelled turtle ancestry about 100 million years ago.

The large, powerful snapping turtle (*right*) is much maligned because of its prehistoric appearance and carnivorous eating habits.

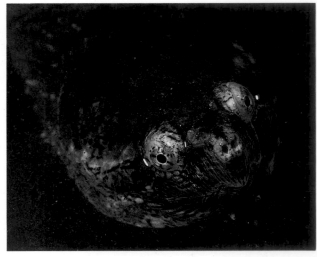

The pretty painted turtle is about five inches in length. Because of its liking for soft-bottomed, weedy ponds and marshes, it sometimes is called the mud turtle.

Like all tree frogs, the Pacific tree frog (*above*) can change colour in minutes to blend with its surroundings.

The lively, colourful little leopard frog (*right*) is familiar to most people. It is commonly found in lakes, rivers, ponds, marshes and meadows.

To frighten its enemies, the northern roughskin newt (*above*) throws its head back, twirls its tail and exposes its brightly colored belly.

The shiny-black, double-crested cormorant (*following pages*) is the only one of its family found inland. Unlike most waterbirds, this cormorant lacks plumage oils and spends long periods on land drying out its wings.

With its crested iridescent green
and blue head, the wood duck is
the glamor bird of the waterfowl.

Much maligned by swimmers, the timid water snake (*above*) is non-venomous and will glide away rapidly if approached.

The venomous eastern Massasauga rattlesnake (*left*) is found in the northeast. It will not attack unless provoked or accidentally disturbed.

THE MOUNTAINS

Mountain animals are well adapted to their rugged alpine homes. Bighorn sheep have roughened foot pads to provide good traction on rocky terrain. Mountain goats can jump ten feet from one ledge to another with ease. And the keen-sighted cougar is an excellent climber, making its lair in rock crevices.

The regal trumpeter swan (*left*), until recently nearly extinct, breeds locally from southern Alaska to Wyoming.

Dall's sheep prefer more north-
erly mountains than bighorn
sheep. They frequent alpine,
tundra slopes in summer,
southern-facing, lower slopes
in winter.

The graceful and aristocratic
Dall's sheep is a favorite among
big-game hunters.

The largest cat and among the
most predatory of North American animals, the wary and solitary cougar or mountain lion
(*above and right*) is a rare sight
in its natural haunts.

The mighty grizzly bear (*above and top right*) has earned its reputation as North America's most ferocious and dangerous mammal. Enormously strong and afraid of nothing, it will attack readily if provoked.

The hoary marmot (*left*) shares the grizzly bear's remote mountain home.

A closer relative of the antelope than of sheep or goats, mountain goats (*following pages*) are expert climbers, scaling rocky cliffs with stiff-legged ease.

Larger and stockier than eastern white-tailed deer, mule deer (*above and right*) live in the foothills and mountains of the West. In summer, the bucks' antlers grow "in the velvet" (*above*), a soft, protective skin. They are shed each spring.

In the late fall, the giant kodiak bear (*following pages*), a subspecies of the grizzly, stocks up for its long winter hibernation by catching hundreds of salmon migrating up the coastal rivers of Alaska and northern British Columbia.

Apart from his herd of mountain goats, a shaggy billy (*above*) surveys his territory from a pinnacle where he is secure from his enemies. Mountain goats live in the most rugged terrain imaginable (*right*), even the most steep and exposed.

Kodiak bears (*above and right*) can weigh 2,000 pounds, more than twice the weight of the average grizzly. Kodiak and polar bears vie for the distinction of being the largest land carnivore in the world.

Sure-footed and agile, Rocky Mountain bighorn sheep can scramble up mountain slopes as fast as 15 miles per hour. The ram (*above*) is a majestic animal. His crowning glory is his massive, curling horns.

The mother ewe (*right*) bears her young on a steep, rocky cliff ledge near a mountain stream.

THE ARCTIC

No one fully understands the boom and bust life cycles that are the norm for arctic animals. But every species hardy enough to cope with life north of the tree-line runs a risk of drastic fluctuations in its population when the finely tuned balance between numbers and food supply falls out of sync.

Restless nomads, barren-ground caribou (*left*) migrate in mass herds over the arctic tundra in search of food.

Scoters are large, black ducks
with distinctive bills. The surf
scoter, smaller and more agile
than most scoters, spends much
of its life at sea, diving into the
rising crest of a wave to catch its
food at the surf line.

Phalaropes are small, swimming sandpipers, noted for their sex-role reversal. The female red phalarope (*above*) is larger and more flamboyantly colored than the male and takes the lead in courtship, leaving the male to incubate her eggs and care for their young.

When on the move, caribou (*above*) eat on the run and readily ford streams and rivers.

A protective brown and red in
summer, a snowy white in winter,
the willow ptarmigan (*left*) is
well adapted to the arctic tundra.

A small, arctic sandpiper or peep, Baird's sandpiper (*above*) prefers drier terrain than many of its cousins.

Unlike any other gull, the ivory gull (*right*) is entirely white, perfectly adapted to its High Arctic home.

A slim aristocrat among birds, the red-throated loon (*above*) haunts remote, arctic tundra ponds, in keeping with its wild, mournful wail.

The common eider (*right*) is a large, diving duck of the arctic coastline, valued by the Inuit for its eggs and down, which is extraordinarily warm and soft.

The king eider drake is an exceptionally handsome bird, its striking bill extending like an orange shield across the front of its head.

Walruses (*left*) are gregarious animals, spending much of their time huddled in densely packed groups on ice floes or, in fine weather, on rocky promontories.

The male walrus (*above*) can weigh a ton and a half. His tusks, which he uses to rake the sea floor for food, can grow to two feet in length.

The white or beluga (Russian for whitish) whale (*above*) is a small arctic whale believed to be a primitive dolphin.

White whales are sociable, swimming in small groups or in schools (*right*) of 100 or more individuals.

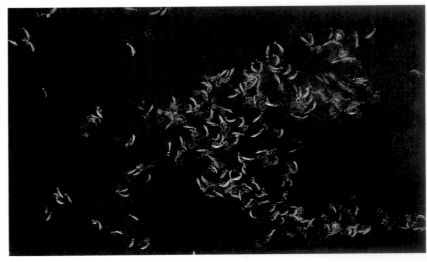

Called sea canaries in early whaling literature, belugas are vocal whales, uttering a variety of puffs, whistles and squeals.

Harp seals are the beautiful, fur-bearing seals that are the basis of the sealing industry and have become an international political issue. They seek the open channels between ice floes to breathe.

Named for its bizarre-looking inflatable crest or hood, the male hooded seal (*left*) can weigh up to 900 pounds.

Hooded seals are aggressive, an uncommon trait among seals. Above, a female defends her pup.

When attacked, musk-oxen (*following pages*) form virtually impregnable, defensive circles around the cows and calves in the herd.

The beautiful, little arctic fox (*above and left*) finds its way to the most remote arctic islands, after trailing polar bears far out onto frozen seas to feed on seal carcasses discarded by them.

The primitive, shaggy musk-ox (*far left*) is the undisputed emperor of the land of ice. Stubborn, savage, and cantankerous, he has survived for 20,000 years.

Unlike other owls, the stunningly beautiful snowy owl (*top*) perches in exposed places. Every fourth year or so, when the population of lemmings, its staple food, declines, the snowy owl wanders south from its arctic home. Immature snowy owls (*right*) are seen further south more often.

The gyrfalcon (*above*) is the largest of the swift, powerful falcons. In the eastern High Arctic, it turns white during the breeding season.

The long, spirally twisted horn of the male narwhal (*above*) is the source of the medieval myth of the unicorn. How this whale of eastern arctic seas uses this strange tusk is still unknown.

Like the lemming, the Arctic hare (*right*) undergoes dramatic cycles. After a two- to three-year population explosion, the intense competition for food and shelter causes many literally to worry themselves to death.

The lemming (*above*) is famous for its suicidal mass migrations. About every four years, thousands erupt from overcrowded burrows and run until they collapse, are overtaken by predators or drown in the sea.

Polar bears (*following pages*) frequent the southern, broken edge of the arctic ice pack. These enormous, stolid beasts can weigh 1600 pounds.

Polar bears prey on seals, young walruses, seabirds and fish. Two polar bears (*above*) devour a bloody seal carcass.

White-headed glaucous gulls (*right*) are a rare sight even on a High Arctic ice floe.

Polar bears ordinarily are solitary animals. They live on icefields as easily as on land, crossing ice too thin to support a man by spreading their legs to evenly distribute their weight.

Herring gulls stand silent watch
on a lonely arctic sunset.

PHOTO CREDITS

INDEX